A YEAR IN MY NEW ENGLAND GARDEN

ANNEMARIE GODSTON

Given by the author

ISBN:1503130320
ISBN-13:9781503130326

This book is dedicated to my mother, Musse Jensen, who taught me to love the beauty of a garden. It was by her side that I learned to properly dig and plant. It was through her eyes that I was introduced to the loveliness found in a blossom.

CONTENTS

ACKNOWLEDGMENTS

First and foremost, I must acknowledge my mother who started me on this lovely gardening "hobby".

I came to this point through the encouragement of my children, Pete, Greg, and Christa, who are always so supportive of me.

Without the understanding and support of my husband, Joel, I would never have taken the time and effort needed to accomplish this labor of love.

INTRODUCTION

<u>WHY GARDEN?</u>

Well, mostly because you love your garden!

But it also does wonderful things for your mental state, your physical state and even your emotional state! Why else would we have been doing it all these years? We truly love to get our hands and jeans dirty. Dirt under the fingernails tells the world we are gardeners, and of that, we're proud! I can remember my mother wore red nail polish, not to look sexy, but to cover the dirt that hid under those nails; the dirt that refused to wash, or be scrubbed out. Garden dirt is tough to remove!

How wonderful it is to have perfect strangers walk up to you when you're out there on your knees and tell you how great your garden looks. They love to see it every time they pass by. In fact, many people choose to walk that way BECAUSE of your garden. That is a genuine HIGH! Along those same lines, how many folks have you gotten to know because of your garden? It's like little children and puppy dogs... everyone stops to admire them. It is a way to get to know new people and connect with your neighbors.

For those of us who are aging, even when we were younger and able to garden easily, we came inside and ached with sore muscles. We expected that, it kind of came with the territory. Unlike now (at a more "advanced" age) it didn't create limits, it just made us stiff for a few hours. At any rate, it tells you that when we garden, we are actually exercising! It's GOOD for us, as long as we know our limitations and stop before we get SORE, or begin to really hurt. We are working those muscles, and that's good!

Let me add at this point, that you will find repetitions of garden chores-month to month, I have done this intentionally, because there is overlap. If a gardener looks for particular chores in one month, not referring to the months either before, or after, they might miss something important!

IS THERE A GARDEN IN JANUARY?

Every book has to have a beginning. One having to do with a calendar should begin in January. To me, the gardening year really begins in April, when the majesty of the garden begins to show it's wonderful face.

But, I digress. It is January. It's dark; it's dreary; it's cold; perhaps snowy. But there are always the birds. There really is nothing you can do outside right now, unless the snow is soft enough and you can knock it off your shrubs and bushes. Ice would probably be the demon of the day. Do NOT try to knock the branches during bitter cold, or if there is ice on those branches. They will BREAK, which would not be a good thing.

Living in the north, we should expect to see snow in the winter. Perhaps there is a LOT of snow out there!

What happens in the garden with all that snow? Is it good, or bad for our gardens? It actually is both, so let's talk about that.

Snow is mostly good. However, one of the bad things is that it can break weaker branches on shrubs and small trees. I advise people to take a broom, or shovel HANDLE and gently bump the branch you want to clear. That will make the snow cascade off. If it doesn't, stop! You don't want to cause any more damage. Branches can break under a heavy snow load. If it ices up, you could be in trouble.

We all know that sometimes it is really cold, and there is very little if any snow cover. That is not a great thing for our plants, trees and shrubs. The snow provides a layer of insulation...and protection from a drying wind.

In a northern climate the plants are far better off with a snow cover. It helps keep the ground at a constant temperature. It also offers support for fragile stems and trunks protruding from the ground.

The only good thing that I can think of during snow-free times is that little rodents that tunnel around in the snow can't really do that if there is no snow. They spend all winter figuring out which tender shoots they can use for food. I guess that says there's a good and a bad side for just about everything.

But, let's talk about the good things.

Snow definitely insulates and protects the plants. That is why Eskimos live in snow houses. It's warm in there. It also protects the ground from the repeated freezing and thawing that can play havoc with roots, bulbs and even seeds.

When the snow melts, it usually melts slowly, releasing liquid gently into the ground. This is good for the plants that have been doing without hydration all winter long.

When you shovel, you can put the excess snow on plants that are living in sheltered places (like under the eaves-as long as you don't get too close to the house with the snow. You don't want water to become an issue inside as it melts.)

If you have a spot in the garden that becomes a mud-puddle, or quagmire in the spring and summer, avoid putting excess snow there, but instead, make plans for a "rain garden" in that spot.

Often we think a plant is failing, or dying because it is suffering from the cold. Most of the time that is not the case. What does happen is that the plant, just like us, breathes. It, however, breathes through its leaves. As it does that, it is losing moisture. So if this moisture is allowed to leave the plant without getting any re-hydration, the plant dries out. A plant needs to be sheltered from wind because the wind can speed up that drying process. This is why the snow is good. It helps by hydrating the plant all winter, while protecting it from the wind. The wind is why gardeners often shield their shrubs with burlap.

If you get a warm spell, it is helpful to give a shrub a good long drink. I realize that's not always possible because the hose is put away, and who needs the possibility of an icy spot. But, it does show you that if there had been snow under that shrub, it would have melted during the thaw and given the plant a drink.

So, don't worry about snow in the garden. It's mostly a good thing!

Pruning trees is always a conundrum of sorts. When is the best time to do your tree pruning? It depends on where you live and what hardiness zone your trees occupy. If you have specific questions about your own location refer to the Extension Office of the Land Grant University of your state (usually titled, "University of "state name" extension service"). They will be very helpful.

My personal opinion is that the best time to prune is in the winter. However, there are a few things that you have to think about before you make this decision. In mid-winter the snow may be deep; temperatures horrendous; and your spirit, unwilling.

This pruning is usually termed, "late winter pruning", but in late winter the sap is already beginning to run in trees like maples and birch (think maple syrup and birch beer. Both are tapped in February and March.) Also, there are those gardeners who feel cutting hard, frozen wood can damage the cells, making it difficult for the cut areas to heal properly. Another complication is that severe pruning can cause a flush of growth the minute temperatures rise. If it's a blooming tree that may flower, the new growth will be damaged and your fruit curtailed. So, hold off on pruning them until March or April.

One of the reasons mid-winter is a good time to prune is that you can see what needs to be done since there are no leaves on the branches. The shape of the tree becomes obvious. You can also, quickly, pick out the broken branches.

As you can see, this is not a simple decision. I personally wait until a warm "January Thaw" type day (whether in January, February, or even early March), and then get my tush out there!

GREEN UP YOUR LIFE

I once, not too long ago, took a course titled "Green up your Life" at the ILEAD program of Dartmouth College, in New Hampshire. I learned a lot about how to make our lives more energy efficient.

We discussed Passive Solar Energy. This is when you are able to heat the space where you live without any mechanical assistance. It means you try to encourage sun to stream into your home on a cold day. Not only should it stream in, it should warm up something in that room that will be able to absorb the heat and release it later, when the sun settles down for the night. If the sun hits the hard mass of the fireplace, or a piece of furniture that gets warm as a result of the sun hitting it, you're golden!

As gardeners we can take note of the fact that by planting deciduous trees outside sunny windows, we keep the house cool in the summer because that leaf cover produces shade. When the leaves fall in the autumn, the sun is allowed to flow into our homes adding to the warmth of our house.

We can also plant evergreens around the north side of the house to shield it from winter wind and snow. These are little things, but they can make a huge difference!

GARDENING CHORES FOR JANUARY

- Start looking for those wonderful **gardening catalogues!**

- **Start a gardening journal.** You can use a notebook, a calendar or even a published gardening journal you buy at the bookstore!

- This is a good time to **check old seeds for viability.** While you're there, paste a label on the envelope indicating when they should be planted, and whether they need soaking first. Then **sort them according to that timetable!**

- Your **indoor plants** get pretty dry at this time of year. Try misting them. (Don't mist African Violets, however!) All plants should be watered sparingly during the winter. Standing them in a tray of wet gravel is a wonderful treat for any indoor plants in winter.

- **Turn indoor plants** every week or so in order to keep their growth even, as they will grow toward the sun.

- Check those **indoor plants for insects** and give them a soapy, bubble bath if you find any!

- Remove any heavy snow from **evergreens.** Be careful! If it is icy, wait until the ice melts.

- Try stamping a circle (in the snow) around **the trunks**

of fruit trees, which are vulnerable to rodent damage.

- Put your discarded **Christmas tree** outside to provide shelter for the birds.

- You can also **smear** the discarded Christmas tree **branches with peanut butter mixed with corn meal**. The birds will love it! Remember though that bears and other creatures will love it as well.

- Another use for that tree would be to **cut some boughs off** and lay them on top of your flower beds to add extra protection.

- Keep those **bird feeders** full.

HOW ABOUT FEBRUARY IN THE GARDEN?

I'm sure you are familiar with Ben Franklin's quote, "God helps them that help themselves."

I think that statement really applies to all gardeners, don't you? Every gardener I know does a good job of taking care of themselves and their gardens. If someone else is doing their gardening, it's not really THEIR garden, is it?

Even at this time of year, most gardeners are busy pouring over their gardening catalogs and dreaming of warmer days to come. Some have been outside picking branches of spring flowering shrubs, bringing them inside for the wonderful phenomenon of "forcing". If you do this, you can treat yourself to early spring bloom inside your home. Bring in some branches from flowering shrubs and trees and force them into bloom for everyone's enjoyment!

Some of the best plants to force are forsythia, pussy willow, and witch hazel. These can sometimes be convinced to bloom in as little as a weeks time! If you're willing to wait up to 4 weeks, try apple and, or cherry. Then for a really long wait, for the truly patient gardener, try lilacs. It's not hard at all. Essentially, you cut the branches, stick them in a bucket of water, stand back and the blooms will come.

Of course, we have to assume you are able to get to your shrubs! If you have a lot of snow, remember to gently remove the heavy snow from the branches of your shrubs. The best way to do this is to go out with a rake or some tool with a plain, broom type of handle. Poke the handle end of the tool into the bush, gently pushing the branches so they move and topple the snow off. However, if the branches are covered with ice, DON'T do this. You don't want to break the branches. If there's ice, you're better off just waiting and letting nature melt it off. Sometimes you also need to know when NOT to do something!

Something else we might think of in these "off" moments in the garden is the possibility of installing a "Rain Garden" somewhere in the garden, maybe this year!

A rain garden is NOT a pond! They are not designed to hold water permanently. An effective rain garden depends on water percolating into the soil of the garden. They are actually miniature, temporary wetlands planted with native plants.

A rain garden is an attractive, low maintenance landscaping feature planted with perennial native plants naturally adapted to wet conditions. It allows plants, bacteria, and soils to clean the water as it seeps its way into the ground. This usually takes only a few hours. It is a way for homeowners, as well as businesses, to participate in the reduction of polluted runoff. It is an infiltration technique in the form of a planted depression, designed to soak up storm-water run-off from impervious surfaces such as roofs, driveways, patios, walkways, basement sump pumps, and even compacted lawn areas. Storm water runoff is considered one of the main sources of water pollution nationwide. Rain Gardens just might get storm water management out of the curb and gutter, and into our front and back yards. The water is held in the landscape so plants can take it in and soak into the ground instead of flowing into the street and down a storm drain or drainage ditch.

Rain Gardens can cut down on the amount of pollution reaching creeks and streams by up to 30%. They prevent storm water from becoming contaminated with oils and other chemicals in the first place. The soil, mulch and plants, actually remove and break down pollutants from the water, as it percolates through the soil, on it's way to become groundwater.

These gardens can be small, informal, homeowner style gardens; large complex bio-retention gardens; or anything in between. It might seem that this is a very small contribution, but collectively, rain gardens can produce water quality benefits. These gardens are a sustainable way to recharge our water in a way the current system does NOT. Planting a small rain garden somewhere near your home helps lock rainwater in the ground.

SPECIFIC GARDENING CHORES FOR FEBRUARY

- Bring home some wonderful **blooming flowers** to enjoy around the house!

- Look around the garden (if it isn't covered by snow) and be sure none of your perennials have **been heaved out of the ground** by frost. If they have and the soil is willing, press them back down.

- Remove any **heavy snow** from the evergreens.

- This is the time to get out and take a good look at your trees to see if they could stand some **pruning**. It is easy to see whether there are broken or diseased branches now since there are no leaves. Remove them.

- Are you ordering from those **catalogs**? This is the time to plan on making your dreams come true! At least in the garden.

- As you look around the neighborhood, make note of **plants that have "winter interest".** Find out what they are and plan to add them to your garden when the weather is better!

- **Trees are easy to identify** in the winter because all the leaves are gone. However, you have no leaves to help you identify them either...so go to the book store and buy a Winter Tree Identification Guide. It's kind of fun identifying trees by their shapes, and the kids love doing it as well.

- If you haven't done it already, **sharpen those tools**-and while you're at it, organize them as well.

- Before you know it, it will be time to roll out the **lawn mower**. Has it been serviced? Get it to the shop before everyone else beats you to it.

- If you have **grapes, prune the vines now**. If you wait until it begins to warm up, they will "bleed".

- If you start **vegetable seeds** this month or next, try using clear topped take-home trays in which you get leftovers from restaurants. They work really well!

- **Force some of your spring blooming twigs** for indoor color. Try fruit trees, forsythia, dogwood, pussy willow and quince. Just bring them inside and allow them to sit in a large vase, or bucket filled with water.

- Keep **those bird feeders** full.

- Be sure to keep the **leaves of indoor plants** "dusted". It helps to wipe them with a damp cloth to keep the pores open.

MARCH IN THE GARDEN

THE SOIL IN YOUR GARDEN

During these days of anxious waiting to get out into the garden, you should be thinking and educating yourself, about SOIL!

If your soil is good, your garden will be wonderful too. This applies to flowering plants, as well as vegetables. The plants take their nutrients from the soil. It's just like humans. We are what we eat. Plants work the same way.

It's so easy to get that soil where it should be. There are organisms that help the soil thrive, thereby helping every plant that grows there.

The first place to start is with a compost heap or bin. Do all the research you can on compost. You will soon be convinced, as are all serious gardeners, that compost can change your gardening world.

You can start with the simplest of techniques by digging trenches and inserting kitchen scraps-NO fat or cooked items please. You just cover those scraps well with soil and voila, next year you have a row that's soft and nutrient rich! OR, you can make a compost heap where you just pile garden (and kitchen) debris, covering each addition with soil or leaves or something organic; leave it for a season; and next year... another voila! A bigger pile of black gold. This is usually sited in an out of the way spot in the garden.

Then, of course, there's the little more complicated, but neater looking, compost bin. These are easy to make;

look a whole lot better than a pile; and work wonders for the garden!

I promise, when you use compost you will become addicted to the process. Your garden will benefit because the soil, where you apply it, will be so much healthier and able to support wonderful plant materials. There is a reason why they call compost <u>"Black Gold"</u>!

On a different note, have utmost faith that the snow will soon stop and wonderful, spring bulbs will begin to poke their welcome leaves up through the soil! WE CAN'T WAIT!

It is good to be prepared for this eventuality. Go get yourself some markers. Be they metal, popsicle sticks or whatever, it doesn't matter. When your bulbs begin to flower, take a marker and note the color and the name of whatever it is, and poke that into the soil right next to them. As the season progresses and the leaves of those little guys die back, they will get lost in the perennials and annuals you have planted around them. Whatever befalls them, you'll know where they are. There are also those who prefer to put markers where they want to plant more. Whatever works for you...do! Remember, it's YOUR garden!

When fall comes, and it's time to plant more bulbs, you won't forget where you already have them. You will know what colors you can mix and match. You'll know NOT to plant more daffodils right where you already have a ton of them. Instead find another spot where they will make a welcome addition to your garden.

OR, if you had a very prolific bunch, you can dig them up and separate them without having to dig up an acre and a half!

GARDENING CHORES FOR MARCH

- Be sure to fertilize that **poinsettia**.

- Check your **stored bulbs** to be sure they're not being eaten by mice.

- Also, remove **forced bulbs** from cold storage. Put them in a cool place until they begin to sprout, then bring them to the place you want them to bloom.

- This is a good time to buy **summer blooming bulbs**.

- **Start seeds** inside.

- **Begonias** can be started in peat moss.

- If you haven't done so yet, **start planning a new garden**!

- This is a good time to send in a **soil sample** for testing...if you can get to it!

- If you have a lawn, this is a good time to send the **mower** out for a tune-up.

- **Fruit trees should be prune**d of dead and diseased branches. After checking a reference book, give them a general pruning as well.

- It is time for **Dormant Pruning**. This is the process whereby you prune the trees while they are in a dormant (non-growing) state.

- Keep your pruning shears away from **spring blooming trees and shrubs**, except to snip a few for inside forcing! (Although you should certainly remove dead and diseased branches.) Some good forcing candidates are: cherry, apple, dogwood and forsythia. Just remember that whatever you cut off now will not be blooming in a few months!

- Cut **back woody perennials** like artemesia, lavender and russian sage to about 6 inches from the ground.

- About **pruning shears**...sharpen them before using.

- If any of your plants are **frost-heaved**, gently push them back into the ground.

APRIL IN THE GARDEN

I think one of the most wonderful things to do in your garden is to relax and enjoy it. I accomplish this frequently by taking a walk from one end of the garden to the other. Depending on what I find to do there, it takes between 10 minutes and an hour. It's a time to reconnect and just deal with very tiny, little issues. I don't need to be in gardening togs. All I need to take along is my pruning shears, a trowel and my gardening gloves ON my hands. Although I must admit, often I take that walk without benefit of any of those. I always regret leaving them in the garage because I come back with dirty hands, grubby fingernails and having left some obvious little tasks for another day.

It's a time to see how everything is growing. Is there a broken branch on the lilac? Snip it off! Has a new weed sprung up between the daffodil leaves? Yank it out! Are the lilies coming up strong and prolific? Enjoy their presence!

I talk to my plants. I encourage them like a mother. I help them deal with small issues before they become large. I "neaten up" their environment. I watch the bees collect pollen. I enjoy the occasional hummingbird flitting around. I jump and then smile when a toad or snake surprises me. I am so happy to see them in the garden because I know they are among my biggest helpers.

I am disappointed to see something fail. When that happens I pull it out, and go on.

I have to say a few more words about composting again. April is the time to start the yearly spring chore of emptying the primary (working) compost bin.

Let me attempt to explain. I have 3 bins, side by side. The large, primary, working bin is to the far left of the bunch. It's made of cedar slats. Next to that I have two smaller bins made of cement blocks. It's all a very simple affair.

The far left one is the "working" bin. Next to that is the one where I dump the stuff from last year's working bin that "hasn't completely broken down". I figure it's full of all the good "bugs" needed to keep the pile working. The farthest one to the right is the "finished compost" from the bottom of the bin. That's where I take compost for the garden.

The far left one is where I dump all my yard waste and kitchen scraps (sans cooked or fatty material). Each time I put some new stuff in there, I take a shovel full of the middle bin's contents and spread over it. It covers and adds working organic "stuff". This makes the whole procedure very easy and do-able. The toughest part of composting, for me, is this spring reshuffling of materials.

HOW "GREEN" IS MY VALLEY? GET PERENNIALS!

I read an article the other day that was absolutely eye opening. It suggested that we can actually "green up" our gardens! Think about that. We are always thinking in an ecologically sound manner, aren't we? We compost; we try to use mulch in order to conserve water; we think about xeriscaping and rain gardens. However, have you thought about this?

Forget the annuals! Every year when we buy dozens of new annuals...they all come in plastic containers which need to get disposed of somehow. Then the annuals need to be watered and tended to all summer long. In the fall, they die. Next year we start the whole process over again.

If, on the other hand, we buy perennials (or get some from friends), we dispose of ONE pot. Then after the plant is established, it needs much less water. It comes up again next year, and actually gives us the opportunity of sharing OUR perennials with friends because the plants get larger and fuller. Fewer pots go in the landfill; less water is expended; we get to share with friends; AND we have beautiful perennials that may cost a bit more when purchased, but last for MANY years.

The moral of the story? Forget some of those annuals and get perennials!

GARDENING CHORES FOR APRIL

- This is a good time to get that **soil tested**. Then there will be time to amend it before the season gets into full swing!
- Edge your **flower beds** to rid yourself of invading lawn rhizomes. Toss the edgings from this into the compost.
- **Rebar**, the steel bars used to reinforce concrete and masonry, **make great garden stakes**. They're inexpensive, strong and durable and they come in a variety of sizes. You can find them in any building supply store.

- Start up your **lawn mower** so you know it doesn't need a trip to the repair shop before grass cutting time. Also, be sure the blades are SHARP.
- Sharpen your **other tools** while you are at it!
- The **lawn** would appreciate a good fertilizing at this time.
- **Avoid working the soil** unless it breaks up in your hand as you squeeze a lump of it.
- **Turn your compost** (assuming it is no longer frozen!)
- **Hummingbird**s begin to appear this month in some places. Clean the feeders and hang them for the "early birds"
- **Sow peas** in the ground as soon as the frost is gone
- Continue with the **tree pruning**. Get rid of dead and diseased limbs
- As soon as your **shrubs are done blooming**, prune them as well.
- You can **prune your berry bushes**-check a reference book
- This is a good time **to pull out weed trees** and old bramble branches. They tend to yank out easily because the soil is still soft and moist.
- Remove mulch from **strawberrie**s
- Put your **trellis systems and peony supports** into place.
- **Pansies and other cold weather annuals** can now be planted outside
- It is the time to **divide and plant perennials** as well as cutting any of last years remaining growth away. It's known as good housekeeping in the garden!
- If you have any **bare root plants** going into the garden, soak them overnight before planting. Also be sure to trim off any super long or broken roots.

- If you winter mulch your garden beds, begin to **remove mulch when forsythia and daffodils bloom.**
- Try planting **scented flowers** near walks!
- It's probably a good time to **remove bird feeders** to discourage those bears (if you have them)!

MAY IN THE GARDEN

Some people sing and dance in the rain, but we're gardeners, so we go out and work in the garden! If you haven't done it yet, get with it!

I know that APRIL is when it usually rains, and March is a bit chilly, so let's approach this now when it's a bit more tolerable in the garden, and then remember it all summer long!

When it's raining, the garden is a wonderful place to be for any number of reasons.

- There usually are **NO** bugs!
- If you're bothered by the heat when you garden, this will be perfect, because it's cooler.
- You probably can get away with not watering newly planted things for a bit.
- The soil stays where you **PUT** it!
- The shock to newly planted materials is so much less.
- No one will bother you!!!!
- Everyone will think you're crazy (which you knew already.)
- This is the best time of all to do your weeding. They almost fly out of the soil!
- Other gardeners will know now that you are serious about this.

There you have it. Now, go on out. Put on you grungiest clothes and boots. Find an old rain jacket, because if it isn't old when you start, it surely will be when you finish. Then be ready to feel like an 8 year old kid, because you will be having fun playing in dirt that is less than dusty. After doing it a few times, you'll grow to enjoy it. **The reason you'll enjoy it is because it really IS the best time to garden.**

PRUNING

Here are a few words about pruning. This is something that comes to the fore about this time of year.

One Sunday, as I sat listening to the sermon in church, the minister talked about "pruning the vine". He was of course, not talking about pruning "literally" but rather in the biblical sense. Being me, my mind began naturally to wander to pruning in MY garden. The minister talked about how he (as a person) had NO interest really in gardening, and if he did, he wouldn't have the slightest clue about how to PRUNE! I'll bet a lot of you, my readers, suffer from similar apprehensions. So, let's deal with your "real" garden, with it's "real" need where PRUNING is concerned. Here are some pretty basic and simple "clues" for pruning.

For instance, why even prune?

- To make your garden, shrubs and trees look the way YOU want them to look!
- To keep that plant healthy
- To control rampant or unattractive growth
- To improve the quality of flowers and fruit

There are some VERY basic things you need to remember before you pick up those pruning shears, loppers or pruning saw.

- Are those tools CLEAN? It doesn't hurt to dip the cutting surfaces in some alcohol or common household bleach to get rid of any "nasties" lurking there.

•What plants are you thinking about pruning? If it is a spring blooming shrub like a lilac, rhododendron, azalea, etc. WAIT until it's done blooming! Why cut off those pretty flowers??? You can certainly cut them to bring into the house and enjoy them, but don't prune until the shrub is done pleasing your eyes and nose.

• If it blooms at the END of the season, like late summer or autumn, it's OK to prune as early in the spring as possible. The reason for this is that early blooming shrubs bloom on last year's growth, and you don't want to remove that growth before it has an opportunity to bloom. Late bloomers usually bloom on THIS year's growth. By pruning (very) early you will encourage new growth and lots of bloom!

• OK, you're now ready to cut, right?

• Look at the shrub or small tree and remove any DEAD, DISEASED, or DYING branches.

• THEN, remove any branches that are growing into the center of the bush. The reason you remove them is that they stop the breezes from getting into the center. If the bush is crammed with leaves in the center, it is vulnerable to fungus and mold, disease and bugs. However, cutting all that stuff out, allows the plant to get some good ventilation and some welcome sun penetrating into the tree.

• Now, cut off any branches that are growing straight UP. They are usually "water shoots" and are unfruitful. (Don't even ask why. Some things are just "understood"! Or to put it another way, I haven't got a CLUE!)

- You're almost done... but now look for branches that are rubbing against other branches. That rubbing will cause an abrasion, which will get raw and very vulnerable to disease. Decide which branch looks best and cut out the other one.

- BY THE WAY-when you cut, cut where the branch joins the next largest branch, back toward the shrub/tree. DON'T make stumps! Cut close to the main branch. Make it LOOK good!

- When you're done with all this, stand back and see how the shrub looks. This is the time when you can attempt to make it look the way YOU want it to look; the way it is most attractive in your garden and it's surroundings. Then just cut out the branches you don't want. Again, don't leave stumps and CERTAINLY DON'T TEAR ANYTHING. The cut should be as clean, and sharp, as possible.

- This doesn't cover EVERYTHING, but it's enough to get you started. .

By the way, remember the disinterested minister? I did give him a few basic clues about pruning, after church. He laughed and said he'd give me a call if he needed something done in his little parsonage garden! I guess I haven't converted him to gardening. :-)

DOUBLE THE RAIN

I have a little technique that I use with my compost. It can be used throughout the garden as well. It allows you to double the amount of rain you get!

I have one of those big colorful, plastic tubs with the rope handles standing right next to the compost bin. When it rains, the tub accumulates water. When it's done raining, I just dump that extra water into the compost bin. Since I've started doing this, the compost has never dried out. I used to drag the hose to the compost and water it to keep it moist. No longer! This works like a charm and it doesn't take a drop from our water system!

I see NO reason why this couldn't work in the garden as well. Put a few of the tubs in various places in the garden, maybe behind a shrub. Then after it rains, just empty it on the plants that need it most.

I will give you one cautionary note however. Mosquitoes breed in water, so don't let that water just sit there...you won't be happy!

GARDENING CHORES FOR MAY

- **Tulip**s should be dead-headed(remove spent flowers, leaving foliage.)

- The **grass** can be mowed when it reaches 3-4 inches (sorry, but it IS that time again!) When you do cut it, set the mower to 2 1/2 to 3 inches.

- Hold off **mulching** until the soil is warm, or you'll just keep the cold in!

- You can now **plant lettuce, beans, corn and carrot seeds** right in the soil.

- **Tomatoes** can be planted when the lilacs bloom. You might sprinkle a teaspoon of Epsom salts into the hole where they go to provide magnesium.

- **Marigolds, zinnias and even nasturtiums** are good to plant in and around your vegetables as well as the flowerbeds. They repel insects

- You can begin to plant **gladiolas** at 2-week intervals.

- This is a good time to **weed dandelion**s, before they flower and set seed!

- You can fertilize any **bulbs** that are up.

- Stake your **peonies** before they get too big. This applies to other tall growing plants. Get the stakes in the ground before they get too tall. (Remember to try rebar.)

- Cut back your **tall perennials** like bee balm and phlox to control their height.

- Harvest **rhubarb** by grabbing it at the base of the stalk and pulling firmly away from the crown, twisting just a bit. Be sure to throw the leaves into the compost as they are poisonous to eat!

- You can prune your **spring blooming shrubs** just as soon as the flowers have faded.

- Dead head your **lilacs**.

- Check your lilies for **red lily leaf beetles**. CRUSH them between your fingers!

- Don't forget to **deadhead your bulbs** as well. Leave the foliage, but take out the spent flower heads.

- Have you got hosta's? Are there **slugs** chewing them? Try this solution, if you haven't already. Combine 9 parts water to common household ammonia and spray it on the hosta just before dark. When the slugs hit this, they will dissolve!

- Check the apple, cherry, and other **fruit trees** for nests of tent caterpillars. As soon as the tender, new leaves emerge, so will the caterpillars. Their destruction is just awful! Bt will work if you can get it up there. I also understand that the Praying Mantis is a big time enemy of tent caterpillars. Perhaps you should order some of those! They should be released into the affected tree at the same time the caterpillars emerge. If you place them before their dinner appears, they will find another yard to in which to chow down.

- If you have to spray insecticide, do it AFTER bloom is finished to **protect the bees and other pollinators.**

JUNE IN THE GARDEN

Plan for color all summer!

So many gardeners fall in love with Rhodies and Azaleas. They ARE beautiful, but remember they only bloom for a short time, and then they are green for the rest of the year. Green can be boring in a garden, unless you REALLY work at it! Not only that, these shrubs can become huge, taking up an inordinate amount of space. So, use a few, but don't get carried away. If you really want shrubs, look for ones that bloom at different times. Try Mountain Laurels, Viburnums, Potentillas and Hydrangeas to add to the mix. There are so many beautiful blooming shrubs, if your space is large enough to hold them.   You can then plant perennials between them.

Check out catalogs that tell you WHEN the perennials bloom and what COLOR they are. As one set of blooms fade, another takes over. THAT'S what makes your garden a joy, to say nothing about INTERESTING! For color, be sure to add some annuals. They retain color for the entire summer and once planted are pretty care free, except for dead-heading (removing dead blooms).

Be sure those colors you plant close together compliment each other. Orange and red are sure interesting, but planted together, they can give you a color headache!

Cultivation of Bearded Iris

Bearded Iris are among the most delightful perennials I can imagine! They are beautiful and

34

relatively easy to manage.

As you think about where to place them in your garden, think "SUN". They love to be in full sun. In warmer climates they appreciate a bit of shade. The rhizomes are healthiest if they are exposed to sunshine and air. Whenever I transplant Iris, I separate them and lay those rhizomes on a sunny rock for a day or two to completely dry out before replanting them. They seem to really appreciate the sunbath.

When you put them into the ground, leave the top of the rhizome a bit exposed. If your Irises do not bloom, check to see if the surface of the rhizome is exposed, if you can't see them, scrape off the dirt and I can almost guarantee you will have better bloom.

Iris can be separated AFTER they bloom. Depending on the variety and your own climate, it would probably be either July or August. The reason for this could not be easier. ENJOY the flowers, THEN dig them up and separate them as soon after flowering as is convenient. Remember they need to be established before frost. I would suggest that you finish this chore before mid-September.

They will eventually get crowded and should be separated every 3-4 years. So, take your gardening fork and dig up the whole clump. Check EVERY rhizome for softness or rot. If there is any rot, ruthlessly cut it out, and discard it in the GARBAGE, NOT THE COMPOST. You don't want to put borers or disease into your compost!

Separate all the rhizomes, discarding the old and saving the new and healthy ones. Lay them on a sunny rock and let them dry out. While you're waiting for that to happen, begin to prepare the hole(s) for replanting.

Dig a hole larger than the spread of the roots. In the center of the hole make a hill of soil, so you can put the rhizome on top of it and drape the roots out and down the sides of the little hill. Always pack the soil firmly around the roots after planting, and water thoroughly. They can be planted between 10 and 24 inches from each other. The closer they are planted, the sooner you'll have to go through this exercise again. However, close planting will give a great display. I guess it boils down to how much time you want to devote to separating Iris!

As far as the soil is concerned, Iris like their soil neutral and well drained. When you plant them you can add bone meal, or super-phosphate directly into the soil. Some people wait until the next year to add this. It's pretty much up to you. After they are established any 6-10-10 fertilizer will work well.

Generally the iris borer is the biggest iris pest there is! You may see signs of borers beginning in May or June. You'll see little holes in the leaves that will become larger as the borers grow and get hungrier. In order to keep these 'guys' at bay, trim off any dead leaves in the early spring by tearing them off right down to the rhizome. After the Iris have bloomed, you should cut off the leaves in the shape of a fan, a few inches above the rhizome. This tends to help a good deal. Again, if there's any sign of borers, put the leaves in the garbage, NOT the compost!

Be sure to keep these newly planted Irises gently and deeply watered. Once established their need for water is minimal.

GARDENING CHORES FOR JUNE

- Plant your **window boxes**

- **Prune spring flowering shrubs** when they have finished blooming

- Thin **seedlings**

- Use balanced, organic **fertilizer**s around flowers

- Be sure to **fertilize your annuals with <u>liquid</u> fertilizer**. They'll thank you for it by blooming continuously!

- **Stake** tall perennials and tomatoes

- Use a pine needle mulch for **blueberries**

- Be sure your **lawn mower is set** to cut the **grass 2 1/2 to 3 inches HIGH**

- After the **irises** are done blooming they can be divided

- **Gladiolus** corms can be planted

- **Dead-head** (prune off) spent flowers from plants and shrubs

- **Remove rhubarb seed stalks** as they form.

- Cutting back **perennials** such as dianthus, veronica and other similar **shrubby varieties**, will often produce a second blooming. How great would that be? They'll also look better!

- You can take **softwood cuttings of shrubs** this month right through July.

- You can still **plant container grown shrubs**

- Plant **broccoli** seed for fall harvest.

- If you have a water garden, there's still time to plant **water-lilies.**

- **House plants** can soon be moved outside to a shady, protected spot.

- These same houseplants can be **lightly fed with half strength fertilizer.**

- **Mulch perennials and roses** to keep down weeds and conserve moisture.

- Look for **Japanese beetles** either early or late in the day and shake them into a bucket of soapy water. The reason you don't do it mid-day is because they'll out run you!

- Any **annuals** can be safely set out now.

- If you have an **amaryllis** growing inside, now is the time to move it outside.

- Pinch the leading stems of your **chrysanthemums and asters** to encourage them to be bushier and have more blossoms. Continue doing this every 6 inches or so, as they grow.

- If you have **apple trees**, hang red sticky-ball traps to control apple maggot flies. Small trees can get by with 2 balls. Larger trees should probably have 4-6 balls.

- Stop cutting **asparagus** when the new spears get pinkie-finger thin. Let them grow into ferns instead. It will feed the roots.

- Side-Dress **veggies** to give them a little boost

- Have you got hosta's? Are there **slugs** chewing them? Try this solution, if you haven't already. Combine 9 parts water to 1 part common household ammonia and spray it on the hosta just before dark. When the slugs hit this, they will dissolve!

- Are you remembering to **turn the compost** every once in a while? You should also **wet it down** if the hose is close by. Doing this will help the contents decompose quicker, although it will eventually happen anyway!

- **Cut back any daffodil** drifts as they die down.

- **Order your bulbs** so they arrive in time to plant in the autumn.

JULY IN THE GARDEN

NEW BABY/NEW GARDEN

Why did I name this topic "New Baby/New Garden"? Well, think about it. When you have a brand new baby the doctor checks to be sure all is fine. There are tests to be taken, and analyzed; there are new skills to be learned; there are fun things happening; and grungy chores to be dealt with; but we also look forward to pleasant surprises with a few bumps along the way. Yes, new babies and new gardens are VERY much alike!

Let's start with the tests. They are an important and critical start to that new baby's life. If there are any medications or special cautions to be taken, we learn about them as soon as possible. The same thing applies to the garden. If you're working with a brand new garden, get a soil test done! It will tell you all about the good AND what is lacking in your soil. Contact your State University Extension Service for details. If you tell them what you're planning to plant, they will tell you exactly what to add in order to amend your soil.

With a new baby, you begin to make wonderful plans for that little person. You get a Baby Journal and begin to add photo's and comments about the baby's progress. In the garden, a Journal works very well also. I'd suggest you get (or make) one of them, it will show things faling into place very nicely. Photographs of your garden will be wonderful. Before and after pictures are a great way to track your progress and learning.

Before you bring that baby home, you purchased furniture and other "things" like diapers, clothing, powder, baby oil, etc. etc! The same applies to a gardener. You'll need some tools, small and large to help you manage your new tasks.

Just as you have to change dirty diapers with your new baby, you'll also have to do some weeding, digging and planting in the garden. Some of this you will love, some you may want to delegate to others!

I'm sure you can think of many other comparisons. Realize that just as a baby grows into a wonderful person, your garden will evolve into a place of grand pleasures. Enjoy it!

GARDENING IN THE RAIN

I spent a gray morning at a lecture about political polling. It was very interesting and I learned a lot.

It was pouring rain outside...but cozy inside!

On the way out of the auditorium, the lady I was with commented that the rain saved her from weeding this afternoon.

Hmmmmm..... I was going to give her my lecture on rain and gardening, but I refrained. However, I can give it to YOU again!

As I've said before, when it's raining, it is the very best time to garden, as long as it's not SHEETING rain! You don't want to go out into the garden and walk around in mud. That's not good for the ground, which compacts too easily; OR for you and your shoes and socks! BUT, when the ground is wet, weeds pull out SO easily. It's much better to weed in the rain, or shortly after it's stopped. The ground is soft, and it falls back into place pretty easily.

It's also a great time to plant because the ground is wet, and the plants are so happy to find their way into welcoming soil.

I'm a big advocate of gardening in the rain. Granted it can be a bit cold, and you'll definitely need to take a warm shower when you get back in the house, but, that feels wonderful anyway.

So, don't be put off by a little rain.

GARDENING CHORES FOR JULY

- Order **spring bulbs** now for the best selection

- Fertilize plants growing in **containers**

- Plant **kale** seed directly into the ground for fall harvest

- Sow a fall crop of **peas**

- Pinch **basil** plants to promote bushiness

- If your **vegetables** are not yielding as much as you'd like, plant some nectar producing flowers in the vegetable garden to **attract more bees and other pollinators**. Remember herbs bloom, and go fit right in with the veggies. Here is a short list: umbells (yarrow, dill, carrots, and parsley) marigolds and petunias. They will also help repel harmful insects in your garden.

- Pick the **zucchini** while it's young and tender.

- Put nets over **blueberries** to protect them from birds. While you're there, give them a little fertilizer as well.

- Remove fruiting **raspberry canes** after you have harvested the berries. Once they have given fruit, they will not bear again, so while you can identify them, cut them out!

- Control the growth of **strawberry runners**. If you don't trim them back, they will be all leaves, and no berries!

- **Dead-head** (prune off) all spent blossoms

- It's a good time to **sow seed** of biennials and perennials

- Cut back **delphiniums** when they are finished flowering. Adding a complete fertilizer (for example: 10-10-10) at this time may encourage a second blooming.

- **Chrysanthemums** will give a better fall display if fertilized abit now. You can continue pinching them back until mid-July for more blooms.

- Try planting a clump of moisture loving **Japanese iris** where it can catch the water dripping from your air conditioner!

- **Madonna lilies** should be divided as soon as the flowering period is over.

- **Oriental poppies** may be moved. Summer is the only

time of the year they can be divided successfully. Dig up the roots and cut them into 2 inch pieces and replant them in their new location.

- **Dahlias** require little artificial watering in a normal season, but should be soaked once a week during a drought.

- Water your **roses** at least once a week

- **Floribunda roses** will flower all summer, if the old flower clusters are snipped off regularly

- This is the time for transplanting **iris**. Trim back foliage and only replant healthy, firm rhizomes. Set them close enough to the surface, so the tops of the rhizomes show!

- In fact, this is the best time to **divide all spring blooming perennials**.

- Start cuttings of coleus, geraniums, begonias and other **plants you want inside** for the winter.

- **Snow-in-summer** should be pruned hard, as it makes such rapid growth at this time

- When you trim **deciduous hedges** be sure the sides slope out toward the bottom (a shallow pyramid shape) to be sure that sunlight reaches the base of the plants.

- **Wisteria's** may be pruned now

- Be sure you dead-head all your **daylilies**. They will

attempt to make seeds if you don't do this. You want them to build stronger roots. Daylilies will bloom more profusely next time if you remove spent blooms. Dead heading will also give you the possibility of a "re-bloom"!

- This is a good time to attack **Poison Ivy!** Using **disposable plastic gloves** cut the stems and paint the open wound with an herbicide. Try to do this on a HOT, SUNNY day!

- Have you got **hosta**? Are there **slugs** chewing them? Try this solution, if you haven't already. Combine 9 parts water to 1 part common household ammonia and spray it on the hosta just before dark. When the slugs hit this, they will dissolve!

- When you **weed**, grab the flowering weeds first, so they don't go to seed and spread! Then go after the tallest ones that are taking over your other plants. Pick on the little guys last.

- Watch for **tomato hornworm**, hand pick, and squish them.

August in the Garden

BLUEBERRIES

My husband and I went to a friend's home, which happens to be on the market. We didn't go to visit, because she no longer lived there. No, we went to pick blueberries.

To me, blueberries are heaven, no matter how they are served. I love them fresh off the bush; with cream; in buckles and pies. I just LOVE blueberries!!!

The reason I was able to pick blueberries at this friends home is because a few years previous, I had helped her by pruning her bushes. In lieu of payment, I was given free picking privileges...which is MUCH better; that is until I learned she was moving.

I was delighted to see that the pruning really paid off. The bushes I pruned had a yield FAR surpassing those I had NOT pruned. What a reward that was. It just goes to show that pruning your blueberries REALLY MAKES A DIFFERENCE. Next spring, very early, before they bloom, be sure to prune yours!

WOOD ASHES IN THE GARDEN

We occasionally light a fire in the fireplace this month! It sometimes becomes so cool in the house, that my finger itches to turn up the thermostat. BUT, now is not the time for that. It is a perfect occasion to crank open the flue, throw in some logs, and enjoy a pleasant fire in the fireplace, which is exactly what we do. Of course, then I've got the usual ashes to deal with.

I never throw ashes directly into the garden. I always put them in the compost bin. That way, they add lots of carbon to the pile, get mixed in with good compost and don't overburden the garden soil with potassium, or possibly raise the soil pH. This solution is better, and less messy, than broadcasting ashes around the yard.

So, enjoy the fireplace, and put the ashes into the compost bin. That also makes disposing of the ashes in the winter easier. No need to throw them out in the garbage, just head for the compost with those wood ashes!

EASTERN TENT CATERPILLARS

What ever you call them, they seem to be all over; up in the trees, lower or upper branches and even on my peony! YUK! Where-ever they are, I don't like them. When you look at them up close, they are pretty ugly!

What are they? They are Eastern Tent Caterpillar nests, that appear in crotches or at the end of branches of trees, shrubs, and even my peony! The little caterpillars feed all around those silken nests, sometimes defoliating large parts of the plant.

In the summer the adult female moths lay masses of eggs around twigs. The newly hatched caterpillars are the ones that spin those webs. When it's warm and sunny they are out chomping. The "worms" drop to the soil to pupate and the whole cycle begins again.

There are a few ways to deal with them.

o You can cut the nests, branch and all,

right out of the tree and put them in plastic bags to be dumped into the garbage.
- o You can spray them with Bacillus thuringiensis, while the caterpillars are small. This is a bacterial insecticide that doesn't harm beneficial insects.
- o The other possibility that sounds MUCH better is to plant asters to draw a little wasp that will parasitize Tent Caterpillars. We can help ourselves by planting various forms of plants in the ASTER family (Asteraceae) close to the trees that are affected! The daisy-like blossoms attract little ichneumonid wasps. These little wasps don't bother people at all, but they parasitize EASTERN TENT CATERPILLARS!

The happiest part of that little equation is that it's aster season! Even the wild asters are blooming all over. So, beg, borrow or buy some very attractive asters for your garden. Then plant them relatively near the afflicted trees and hope the little wasps find your garden, and hence your caterpillar laden trees.

Also, if you have them in your trees, try to remove the egg masses when you find them in the winter. That will also help control them.

SOME GARDEN MANNERS

My life has been hectic with summer visitors.

Since we will be moving in a few years, I have been offering to share plants with friends and family. At some point, sooner or later, someone will ask YOU if you'd like to have some plants.

Here are some words of advice so you will be asked back again for plant sharing.

ASK where they'd like to have you take the plants. Then when you locate the clump you'll be working on...ASK again what section of the plant they'd like you to remove.

Once you start to dig, be careful NOT to disturb the plant you leave any more than is absolutely necessary. As you remove the section you're taking, shake the dirt into the hole where you took the plant. There's no reason for you to take the soil...you have your own!

You shouldn't leave any holes, a golfer would call them divots, and a polite golfer always replaces them. Those holes are unsightly, and could be dangerous for a passing gardener. No need for twisted ankles!

Be sure the roots that you've exposed are COVERED! You don't want to harm the plant material you leave behind. This is another reason it's important to shake out that soil.

Always leave the garden in such a way that no one would know a piece has been taken. It may require a bit more time and care, but you'll be invited back to help when those plants need to be divided again. If you are clumsy and selfish, no one will want you back working in THEIR garden!

GARDENING CHORES FOR AUGUST

- **Make notes** on what you need to add to next years garden while you can see what's blooming!

- **Dig potatoes** after the tops have died down.

- Prune off those **strawberry runners** to keep your strawberry bed orderly.

- Plant **fall mums**.

- **Water** any newly planted shrubs and trees.

- **Stop pruning** shrubs.

- **Don't fertilize** anymore until the leaves begin to change color. If you fertilize late in the summer, it causes a flush of growth which will probably be "nipped" by frost. So, hold off a bit.

- **Water evergreens** thoroughly during dry weather.

- **Sow forget-me-not seed**. They make an attractive carpet planting for tulip beds

- This is also a good time to **sow poppy seeds**! August sown seed gives richer-colored flowers, so give that a try.

- Cut off foliage of **bleeding heart**, which has probably become unsightly.

- Apply fertilizer around **peonies** and scratch it into the soil. If you want to transplant or divide them, this would be the time.

- Treat for **Powdery Mildew**. Try this recipe: 1 1/2 tablespoon baking soda, 1 gallon of water and 2-3 tablespoons of horticultural oil. Spray it on all the susceptible plants every other week or so.

- Plant **colchicum**'s and **fall crocuses**.

- Order your **bulbs** if you haven't already!

- Cuttings **from English Ivy** now will produce good house plants for winter.

- Are you remembering the **lawn mower** should be set at 2 1/2 to 3 inches to help the grass stay hydrated? Cutting the grass lower will be very stressful for your lawn!

- Reseed any bare spots in the **lawn** with some mixed grass seed varieties. Be sure to pick a grass mixture that is best for **your gardening zone**.

- If you have **an amaryllis** outside, now is the time to think about bringing it inside.

- Still time to **sow lettuces and greens, carrots, beets and turnips** (don't worry about how small they might be...they ALL taste wonderful while still immature!) Be sure to keep all of these well watered. A bit of mulch will keep the tender roots cool. To help with early frosts, a row cover will help.

- Get some netting over **the blueberries**! Remember the

birds and small animals are great at crawling UNDER and THROUGH the netting. Try staking it so they can't reach the berries from the outside. If they get in, you'll live to regret it. Talk about a mess!!!

- Have you got any **hosta**? Are there slugs chewing them? Try this solution, if you haven't already. Combine 9 parts water to 1 part common household ammonia and spray it on the hosta just before dark. When the slugs hit this, they will dissolve!

- Your plants in **hanging baskets and containers** have been roaring through the nutrients in their soil. It's time to give them a trim and a good feeding to help them continue to flourish.

- It's time to **plant perennials, shrubs and trees**. This will allow them to establish some good roots before the ground freezes.

SEPTEMBER IN THE GARDEN

IT'S RAINING!

Hello! It's raining! That's VERY wonderful for your garden.

At this time of year your plants need to soak up enough water to get them through the winter. This is especially true for your broad-leaf evergreen shrubs. All winter long sun, wind, snow and extreme temperatures will stress them. During this time of stress they will be losing moisture through their leaves. In order to keep them healthy, and have the ability to stand up to this desiccating horror, they need to have a lot of water fed to them while the ground is able to absorb it. Autumn rains are nature's way of helping the world's shrubs and trees make it through the winter.

Remember that if it's not raining where you are, or if the amount you get is not significant, do your shrubs and trees a favor and soak them deeply! Allow the hose to dribble water down to the roots for at least 30 to 60 minutes at a time. Do this during any dry spell in the autumn. Your plants will be very appreciative.

TIME TO PLANT YOUR BULBS

Planting bulbs allows the most wonderful dreaming a gardener has all year. The great thing about it is that come spring, your dreams will come true!

When you order your bulbs, you will find there are a range of prices and sizes. If you're buying tulips, which tend to last just one year, I'd buy the bigger, 'showier ones'. If you're buying daffodil and narcissus, which multiply and continue to prosper as the years go by, I'd aim for the cheaper ones, and get more of them. If you're buying smaller bulbs, like crocus and snowdrops, size isn't an issue.

When planting them, tulips tend to look best in formal beds, where as daffodils are wonderful when allowed to "naturalize". You can do that by tossing them over your shoulder and planting them where they land! How fun is that?

Try to avoid planting bulbs right under trees as the tree roots will interfere with the planting, to say nothing about competing with the bulb for water and nutrients...guess who wins in THAT battle!? They do look great in FRONT of trees and shrubs, which create a wonderful backdrop for them.

When planting bulbs, the general rule is to plant them three times as deep as the largest dimension of the bulb, with the pointy end up. If you really can't figure out which end is the pointy one, try laying them (in the soil) on their side...that will work. Also, toss and work in a bit of bulb fertilizer. The bulbs won't be dug up for awhile, so it will behoove you to give them a good start.

Enough for now on bulbs.

SHRUBS IN THE EARLY FALL

There are a few things you need to tuck into your gardening mind about shrubs in the early fall. Shrubs are a pretty hardy bunch, so they will keep trying to put out new growth. At this time of year, you should be helping them pull up the covers and prepare for a long winters nap! How can you do that?

Begin by NOT doing any more pruning of those shrubs. When shrubs are pruned, they attempt to put out new growth to make up for that which has been lost! If it's cold enough that won't be a problem. But, if we get a few warm days in a row? Whoosh...out come the new little shoots. Then the cold returns and zaps the little shoots. Those new, but dead shoots will sit there all winter and invite disease and insects. Help your shrubs by NOT pruning them until it's cold enough that you know no warm stretches will follow. (This is part of the reason pruning is done right after flowering, or when it is consistently warm.)

The same thing applies to fertilizing. If you fertilize too early in the fall, the plant will try to put out newly invigorated growth. Again, wait until you know it's too late for the shrub to generate new little shoots. That way, the fertilizer will go down to the roots where it will help them strengthen and prepare for spring.

Another thought is to stop picking roses for the table. A rose bush will start to harden off when the hips appear. So let your roses form hips and they will probably do better through the winter!

SHOPPING FOR BIRDSEED

It's getting to be that time again. I have a few chickadees that are visiting my thistle feeder. They NEVER eat thistle seed in the winter at my feeders! They must be early "returners" looking for a handout. They know the location of my feeders...so here they are. The pickings are slim since the finches are the only ones I feed (except Hummingbirds, of course) in the summer.

Anyway, that makes me think of birdseed.

A few years ago, I participated in an experiment for Cornell University Feeder Watch. It was to see what seed the birds actually liked enough to pick and eat, if given a choice. I offered sunflower, millet and mixed seed. There was NO question that they absolutely preferred the sunflower.

Since I don't like the mess created by the hulls, and since the hulls are toxic to the grass they fall on, I now offer ONLY shelled sunflower seed. They love the seed, and no shells are left on the lawn. How much more perfect can that be?

I, of course, also offer the thistle for the finches. Occasionally the nuthatches go to that feeder as well. But, even they much prefer the shelled sunflower. Suet is there for the woodpeckers, and anyone else that needs a little "beefing" up!

I don't put my feeders up until after the local black bears have pretty much found a comfy cave and will leave my feeders alone. That means that it's late October or early November before I begin this process.

ELDERBERRY

I've been looking at the elderberry tree in the back yard, right outside the den window. It's loaded with blue-black berries. I understand they make wonderful jelly and wine, but since I no longer make jelly and have never made wine, I'll leave them for the birds and other creatures that might come along needing a snack.

I loved the little flowers it made in the spring, and now I love looking at the berries.

I can remember one year I noticed that the whole tree was shaking and trembling. It was not windy so I was very perplexed and then I saw a flock of cedar waxwings. They had discovered the berries and were in the process of stripping every single berry off that tree. I've never seen that happen again, but it sure was a fun thing to watch. In about 20 minutes every last berry was gone!

LET'S TALK ABOUT POPPIES

This is the time to begin transplanting, dividing and planting most perennials.

Let's talk about **Oriental Poppies**. They are such beautiful flowers and once established, make for some of the most striking color in the early summer garden.

As with most plants, they benefit from full sun and well-drained soil. It has to be noted that their foliage will die off and look pretty ugly. This is one of those cases where planting them among other plants that come up after the poppies have finished blooming is a great idea. That new plant will cover the dying foliage of the poppies as they go into dormancy. Whether that plant is a perennial, or an annual is of course, totally up to you!

The roots are long and skinny, so a deep hole will be needed to accommodate them. Unlike an iris that loves to be planted in a shallow hole, poppies will complain mightily if they are not planted deeply. In fact, they may just quit altogether (and die)!

Another point to remember is that because the root is fleshy and long, they will NOT do well in wet soil. They will just ROT! So be sure to add some compost or maybe sand to the soil around them if the location tends to become wet. Or better yet, find another spot that is more accommodating.

VEGETABLE GARDENING AND SCHOOL LUNCHES

I've been reading a lot lately about how farms and schools are teaming up to provide more produce for the school cafeterias. It means that our children are getting healthier food, and our farms are able to sell their produce locally. There is less fuel used getting the food to the consumer. Fewer containers are needed, and the ones that are used can be reused on the next trip. There are many more organic farms in the mix, which makes this prospect even healthier!

When the kids know where their food comes from, the food becomes more fun to eat. It could be that the farm supplying the food has a youngster attending that school, which might provide opportunities for trips and tours to the farm, as well as talks by the farmer. To learn that food does not originate in the grocery store is a wonderful lesson.

There are schools that have their own vegetable gardens on the school grounds. The children do the gardening and harvesting. How great is that? The kids find out where potatoes and carrots come from. They see how quickly lettuce springs out of the ground, and how yummy it is when eaten fresh.

If this sort of activity is being debated in your community, encourage it! Go and talk to the Board of Education and while you're at it, see to it your neighbors are aware of the possibilities.

<u>GARDENING CHORES FOR SEPTEMBER</u>

- Seed, or over seed, **new lawns** before the leaves begin to fall.

- **Fertilize** your perennials and shrubs... it will help them make it through the winter.

- To keep your **bulbs** in top-notch condition while giving you lots of flowers, scatter a **5-10-20 fertilizer** on top of the ground above them, scratching it in, if possible.

- **Japanese Beetles** lay eggs at about this time, so treat your lawn with **beneficial nematodes** to control the grubs.

- **Stop pruning shrubs**. Pruning will

encourage new growth, which should be avoided. Any new 'stuff' will be nipped by frost, which is NOT good for the plant!

- If you haven't divided your **herbaceous perennials**, such as daylilies, irises, hostas and peonies, get it done soon. Remember the soil is still nice and warm, even if the temperature drops at night. This warmth allows the roots time to settle in and establish themselves before winter sets in! This is what makes fall such a good time to plant!

- Plant some **fall mums**!

- Hips forming on your **roses** tell the plant to harden off for winter, so stop picking blooms for the table!

- Water your **peonies** and **shrubs** very deeply. It will have to last until spring.

- Put all your **non-diseased** plant debris in the compost bin, adding a bit of soil as well, to help get the chemistry moving!

- If you haven't done a **soil test**... now is the time. Call your local Extension Office for information.

- Dig up your **gladiola, dahlia and tuberous begonia** corms.

- **Lily bulbs** become dormant this time of year, so it's time to move or divide them right now. The bulbs are "fleshy" so treat them gently. Replant them at the same depth they were before. Remember they like well-drained, soft soil. If there are **little bulbs present**, separate them and plant them at a depth of about 3 times their height.

- **Poinesttias** should now be put in their dark corner for at least 16 hours each day in order to set up their bracts to be colorful by Christmas time.

- I suggest you begin **removing blossoms from your tomato plants**. This will tell the plant it's time to ripen up the tomatoes on the vine, and stop putting out more blossoms. (Unless you want green tomatoes, that is!)

- Watch for migrating **Monarch Butterflies** that begin to head south about now to spend the winter in Mexico.

- Also, look for **Broad-Winged Hawks** that are migrating as well.

- Start preparing your **indoor plants** to come inside; being sure they are in before frost. You need to be sure they don't have insects hiding anywhere. You also want to clean off the pots, especially if they were sunken into the soil for their summer sojourn!

- Your **amaryllis** can come inside and go into a dark, cool corner.

- Remove your **hummingbird feeders** at the end of the month, if you haven't already.

- <u>**BULBS! PLANT THEM!**</u>

OCTOBER IN THE GARDEN

A HARD FROST-FINALLY!

One October morning when I woke up and looked out over the deck roof, there it was, the telltale, whitish cloak of frost on the roof! If you can believe it that was the FIRST time I had seen frost this early at our home. Actually, a hard frost in early October is pretty unusual in northern New Hampshire.

When I ventured into the living room and looked out at the garden, the frost was visible again. The hosta and the peony leaves were all very dark green, and looked a bit worse for wear. Yup, they had definitely been nipped by a good, hard frost.

So, winter has definitely begun! There are a few things that bubble right up to my gardener's mind. I need to get those hoses into the garage after being drained. AND I need to get burlap covers on the shrubs I want to protect from heavy snows. The birdbath needs to be taken in, so it doesn't freeze and crack...which I've allowed to happen once too many times!

Then there are the few, left over bulbs I haven't gotten into the soil. It's definitely TIME!

If I still lived in Connecticut, I'd be ruminating about the leaves that continue to fall covering the grass...which is NOT a good thing. However, up here in the North Country, I don't worry about leaves too much. There are a few spots we rake, but generally the leaves are not an issue.

So, I welcome the entrance to another season. It

will be less colorful, but definitely just as beautiful. I tend to leave the flower stalks with their flower heads, containing seeds, alone so the birds can find them. They also add a certain interest to the garden. There are times during the winter that I wonder why it was I left them up. They can begin to look pretty sad, but hey, the birds loved them, so who cares how they look in February?

SNOW IN THE MOUNTAINS

One day we went to Littleton, NH so my husband could go to the camera shop. I, on the other hand, went to the Book Store. After we finished satisfying our needs at each of those places, we decided we'd go to the movies. In order to get to Lincoln, where the movies were, we drove through Franconia Notch. It's a beautiful drive. Among other things it goes right by the "Old Man of the Mountain". Unfortunately, as you probably know, the Old Man fell off the mountain and the spot where his face used to be is now just a bare face of stone on the side of a precipitous cliff. How sad!

However, what was really interesting was that the snowplows had actually visited during the night. We had had a few inches of snow. Also, Cannon Mountain Ski area had snow on all the trails and it looked like January!

What does that have to do with Gardening? Nothing I guess, except that it pretty much marks the end of our "outside" time! There are still a few things that can be tended to, but it is just "tending" time, not "doing" time. Realize that your garden isn't gone, it's just resting, catching its breath, taking a break before beginning up again in the spring.

What you can do is go around and just tidy up. Put debris into the compost heap. Remove all those hoops and poles that supported plants that are now decimated by the frost. Be sure that all your tools are inside AND clean! If the hose hasn't been removed and drained, do that too. It's important to drain it because if you don't, it will freeze and most likely split. Clean off your lawn mower and other garden appliances. If they need some work, get them to the shop now. It's a quiet time for those folks right now. It's after gardening time, and before snowmobile time. Time to sharpen, oil, repair and just clean up tools of all kinds.

NEWLY PLANTED BULBS

Have you gotten those new bulbs into the ground yet? I know you are interested in protecting them from the freeze that is surely coming our way, BUT...

Don't mulch those bulbs quite yet! If you mulch them (or your perennial bed, etc.) too early, the mulch will keep the frost OUT of the soil, and the ground will heave and dislodge those bulbs and roots. So, be sure the ground is well frozen before the mulch goes on. By doing it in this order, the bulbs will be frozen into the soil (which is nature's plan incidentally!) and will not be disturbed during the winter, by freezing and thawing.

If you already have mulch on your garden from earlier this year, that's fine, just leave it there. I'm talking about that EXTRA mulch you put on specifically for winter protection!

FERTILIZING IN THE AUTUMN

You CAN fertilize in the autumn. Often you will read that you shouldn't fertilize at this time of year, and generally that is true.

What happens if you fertilize late in the summer (late August-early September), you could force a flush of green growth. This growth will be very "soft". If you get an early frost, it will be "nipped" and die, stressing the tree, or shrub. Or even grass for that matter!

However, if you wait until after the leaves begin to fall, you'll be close enough to the time of frost that the plant will NOT put out that flush of growth. Instead, it will store that fertilizer right by it's roots, gobbling it up all winter and being ready to burst forth when the spring warmth and rains filter down into the ground.

As I told a gardener that questioned me on this issue, you really have to be keenly aware of your garden and it's microclimate. You are the best judge of when any new growth has stopped and when it would be safe to fertilize. Use that judgment. If you goof, hey, the world won't come to an end. Next year you'll have a better idea. Remember it's almost impossible to kill off a garden in a year! :-)

As far as the grass is concerned, if you do a late fertilization, remember to rake the fallen leaves FIRST! If you don't, it will be a VERY patchy cover...and then when you rake up the leaves, the fertilizer will go with them. This would be a huge waste of money AND fertilizer!!!

AUTUMN LEAVES

Most of our leaves have come off their summer perches. They are finished impressing all of the "Leaf Peepers" in our area, and can now come down to begin their next step in the evolution of things organic. Life is a progression. Nothing is wasted, and no stage is without it's benefits. The leaves have gone from bright green leaf buds to wonderful large summer leaves, green and plump. Then they shed their chlorophyll and take on their glorious autumn colors.

Mustard is what I call the next color stage. The trees seem to be spread with mustard. The leaves come down in the wind and rain, and the rakers come out into their gardens. They come armed with rakes and tarps. The experienced and wary ones, also come with gloves. Not because their hands are cold, but because a rake and leaves usually combine to create some of the most painful blisters on the palms of our tender hands. Of course, if you start with callused hands, the gloves can stay inside until it's really cold outside!

When we lived in the Connecticut suburbs, raking leaves was an annual chore that HAD to be attended to. The leaves were dealt with in three different ways. First they were raked into a tarp and carried into the woods behind our back property line. They remained there in a huge pile. T

By spring, this huge pile had diminished greatly. Every year I added to it. It gradually turned into leaf "mold", which is what you call broken down leaves. It is pretty acid, and has a somewhat lesser place in the garden. The blueberries loved it! I mixed the leaf mold into the vegetable garden to encourage worms and looser soil. I used it to add to the compost pile when the mix was too green. I must admit the kids loved playing in that leaf pile as well, when it was newly replenished.

Then, when there weren't too many leaves left on the lawn, I would just let them stay there, ready to be chopped up by the last few mowings. The lawn mower would cut them up and mix them with the grass. I would mow in such a way that I got rows, which I could finally rake onto the tarp and dump, into the compost bin. The pile would heat up nicely, and be ready to go into the garden come spring!

The last of the leaves, too far from the compost bin or leaf pile, went into the street, right by the curb. A few times every fall "snofalaphagus" (as the kids called it) would come by and suck the leaves up into the town truck, carting them off to the town compost. In the spring we were welcome to go and get as much as we wanted for our gardens. I had my own compost, so I never took advantage of that.

Now, however, we live in the country. The only leaves that get raked are those that accumulate in the driveway. They can be quite lethal when wet and slippery! The gardens just accumulate leaves. I leave them there to mulch the plants. In the spring, I remove them after they've protected the garden all winter.

If you have a lawn, it is important to rake up the leaves. Leaves will mat down and suffocate the grass below. It will stop your lawn from breathing, making it quite vulnerable to different kinds of mold and disease, to say nothing of the insects that will take refuge there!

So, grab the gloves, rake and tarp. Invite the

children to either help (OK, so maybe the word is "bribe") or play in the leaf piles. Some of the happiest memories of childhood are made there. The weather at this time is delightful; working in a sweatshirt and jeans just feels wonderful in the fall; breathing in the cool air is so invigorating. It is all the stuff of joy. Even the occasional blister is worth it. Autumn! It's wonderful!

WATER! DON'T SPRINKLE!

I know I talk about seeing to it that your plants are well watered before they go into a long winter's stress. Then I say, "Don't sprinkle"! Well, there's a method to this madness.

If you sprinkle, the water doesn't get a chance to soak into the ground…and at the same time, you use a lot of water. Instead, lay the hose so the water spills directly onto the ground, right at the trunk of the tree, the stem of your shrub, or in the middle of the clump of your perennial plant. At this point, turn the water on so it just TRICKLES into the ground. This way, it will be absorbed right down to the roots without running off the top of the soil. The smaller the trickle, the better. Let it run for quite awhile, maybe half to three quarters of an hour. If it runs longer, no harm is done. Every drop of water will go directly to the roots of the plant rather than just staying on the top of the soil where it does NO good.

So, that's my watering lecture! Remember do NOT use a sprinkler for deep watering! We are not talking about a lawn, we're talking about shrubs, trees, and perennials.

XERISCAPING

I have read quite a few articles recently about the drought that is affecting many parts of the United States. It is a scary prospect. Many communities are asking people not to use water for anything other than absolute necessities. We are facing some definite climate changes. As gardeners, we can be part of the problem, or we can do something about it.

There are so many gardeners, especially in areas that that are affected by the drought, that really are part of the problem. Instead of choosing plants that can deal with less water, they choose water guzzlers, and then proceed to water them constantly. This is not helpful, and it gives gardeners a BAD NAME! Don't become one of them. If you ARE already falling into that category, try to figure out ways to change your concept of gardening.

Here is a definition you need to pay attention to:
xeriscaping (n. xeriscape)
Landscaping with the use of drought-tolerant plants, to eliminate the need for supplemental watering.

Try to familiarize yourself with that concept. It is NOT only for desert landscapes! We can all benefit from this, from the tiniest gardens to the largest. Join me in being part of the solution and NOT part of the problem!

CLOSING UP THE GARDEN

The weather report claimed that we might just get

some snow! Oh, gosh! I'm not ready!!!!

At any rate, it's time to get to some neglected chores. Turn off the water going to the outside spigot from inside the house. That's always a chore for me because I have to climb up into a bunk bed, remove a ceiling tile and turn off the water while bent over into a ridiculous position! But, it's done.

Next, it is time to remove the hose from the spigot and drag it like a snake down the hill, so it will drain. That is always pretty effective. One end of the hose at the top of the hill, the rest winding downhill and emptying into the ground right at the base of the Mountain Laurel. Then later, I'll have to go out and roll it back up to put it away for it's winter nap.

It's also time to collect the pads from the delightful, summer recliner on the deck. They go into a big, black plastic bag. I tie that up and put it into the storage room to await spring and the next warm nap on the deck!

I tried to buy some suet at the local grocery store for the woodpeckers, but they didn't have any! They had a small package with little chunks that would fall right through the suet feeder...so that will have to wait until I get to the store again and MAYBE they'll have gotten suet in larger pieces.

I put out the feeders for the birds last week and I've gotten the usual noisy Bluejays and a few Hairy Woodpeckers, but nothing else. I wonder where the birds are? I'll have to write to the Project Feeder Watch folks at Cornell to see if there's a reason for that. Usually the birds are there the same day I put the feeders up.

GARDENING CHORES FOR OCTOBER

- You can still plant **spring bulbs**.

- Scatter a **slow-release fertilizer** (formulated especially for bulbs) on top of the soil after planting bulbs. Remember to scatter this fertilizer over other beds of bulbs as well.

- If you have **gladiolus**, this is the time to dig the corms up.

- This is a wonderful time to **fertilize both lawn and garden**

- **Plant** cool and warm-season **lawns**

- Move **worm bins** to basement or garage to maintain at least 40* through the winter months

- Divide and pot a **clump of chives**, bringing them indoors for the winter.

- If you haven't lifted your **dahlias** yet, this would be the time!

- Bring any **plants that are growing in containers** inside for the winter. If they are hardy enough to remain outside all winter, tip the pots on their sides so any accumulated water will drain out. Although they should be able to stand the temperatures, ice can definitely be a problem!

- Be sure to bring **clay pots** inside so they don't freeze, causing cracking.

- Reduce feeding **houseplants** (do not feed dormant houseplants)

- Start a dish of **paperwhites**, and if you want a winter-long indoor display, plant a few more every other week.

- Give your **compost pile** a final turning before it snows.

- Try to keep the **fallen leaves** raked off the lawn. Put them in the compost, shredding them first if possible, or mix them really well as they tend to compact.

- Be sure that you have removed any foliage from your **iris** plants. This foliage, if not discarded, can harbor Iris Borers over the winter. You surely don't want to see them in the spring!

- You can plant **garlic** now for next years harvest. It's the perfect time to order and plant them so they have time to begin growing roots before winter sets in.

- **Mark any perennials** you want to separate so you can find them next spring.

- Clean and oil your **tools** so they won't rust over the winter.

- Plant **trees, fruit trees, shrubs and vines** that arrived in a container, or are balled-and-burlapped. Any other trees can be planted now as well.

- Put some **rodent protection** around the trunks of new trees. This can be in the form of hardware cloth or other materials you can get in the garden center or hardware store for this purpose. It will protect the trunks from damage over the winter from hungry little critters.

- Keep **watering** the shrubs and evergreens.

- Plant **container roses** and prune your **hybrid tea roses**. Start preparing your roses for winter. They should be mulched when the ground begins to freeze.

- If your **roses** had signs of black spot or other foliage diseases you should remove the leaves so it doesn't recur again next year. Once a hard freeze has beaten down your garden, remove the leaves from the affected roses, as well as any mulch that might have remnants of those infected leaves, and throw it into the garbage **(NOT into the compost-you do not want to spread it throughout the garden next year.**

- Cut back your **perennials** and put the foliage in the compost as long is it's not diseased. If there is green at the base, leave about 4-5 inches of leaves.

- Try to leave about 4 inches of stem on any **lilies** you cut back. In the spring, they appear rather late. By leaving some of the stem, you will know where they are hiding in the garden!

- Leave the **ornamental grasses**. They look quite

attractive in the winter garden.

- Sow **seeds for frost-tolerant perennials**

- An **"Anti-Desiccant" spray** can be sprayed on the broad leaved evergreens, helping to slow down the winter drying process. I always spray my Rhodies, Azaleas, and other broad-leafed, evergreen shrubs at this time

- Try using evergreen boughs over your shrubs to provide **winter protection**. The stems can be forced into the ground before the ground freezes, draping their branches over the shrubs.

- This is also when a burlap tee-pee can be helpful. The tee-pee will help keep the snow load from breaking branches. Just remember NEVER use plastic. Plastic doesn't breathe and just like you, a plant needs to breathe!

- As soon as that **first heavy frost is done**, apply some mulch. Not only will it protect the plants from "heaving", but also when it works into the soil, it will add all sorts of needed amendments. (The reason you wait until AFTER the frost is that you want to protect the roots from repeated freezing and thawing. If you put mulch on too early, it will take a long time for the frost to work it's way down to the roots, and before the frost gets there, the ground will heave, unsettling those roots. So, **let the ground freeze**. (The plant can deal with that.) Then AFTER the freeze has happened, keep the ground in a state of "freeze" until the weather warms up enough to thaw right through that mulch. Again, no heaving!)

- Pull out your **annuals** and put them in the compost

- It's time to **store your hoses inside**. Remember to **drain them first** so they don't freeze and split!

- Bring in any **annual geraniums**! Potted and kept in a sunny spot, they will bloom all winter. Or hang them upside down (with the dirt removed) in a cool spot like the garage, or basement.

- **Get those bird feeders up! Be sure you have cleaned them first!**

THE NOVEMBER GARDEN

AGE-WHAT IS IT??

Any time I attempt to define a concept, I always start by defining the words I use, so..

AGE means: "the length of time a thing has existed." Hmmm...is that what I mean?

How about: "the latter period of a natural term of existence?"

or how about: "to mature?" I like that one.

As my eye wandered over the dictionary page it fell on **"ag-ile"**: meaning quick and well coordinated. Hey, that's what I USED to be!!!

My eyes also fell on **"aghast"**: meaning struck with shock, amazement or horror. That's what I am nowadays when I venture out to my garden and realize I just haven't got what it takes anymore.

SO, there you have it...the ages of a gardener. Having been "agile"; beginning to "age"; and then being "aghast" when the old body just doesn't work quite right anymore!

I realize I cannot turn the clock back. I can't make my body agile once again, but I don't want to be aghast either. HOW am I going to deal with that garden that has given me such joy throughout my life? There MUST be a way!

I write my thoughts as they come to me, and then pull them all together.

I am beginning to get some comments from gardening friends who are traveling this road as well. For instance, I heard from a gardener who says he goes EVERYWHERE in the garden with a 5 gallon pail he can turn upside down to use as a prop to get him back on his feet. What a GREAT idea!

IT SNOWED AGAIN!

We got about 5 inches of snow over the Thanksgiving holiday! Everything is beautiful and white. I can say this now. In March, my comments will be otherwise I'm sure!!!

Anyway, seeing the snow created a flurry of activity. There were, as usual, a few chores I neglected to get to. Sure we had warnings about winter. There were the usual minimal snowfalls, but they were just teasers. Just like a lot of gardeners, I refused to believe that this could actually get to the point where we had to SHOVEL!

So, here I am, praying that we'll get a warm spell that will melt the snow and allow me to continue with all seriousness the matter of preparing my garden for winter. So, don't feel bad if you forgot a few pre-winter gardening chores! It happens to all of us. Promise yourself you'll remember next year. Let's see what happens then!

THE WINTER GARDEN

The other day, my husband asked if I was going to leave the plants from the summer up...or cut them down.

I usually leave them up for winter "interest". Not only that, the birds appreciate the flower seeds that are clinging to those dead flower heads. I often see the birds checking them out before they are totally covered with snowdrifts.

My perennial bed is close enough to our country road that the plow also seems to find that piles of snow fit quite nicely over my garden bed. I don't think that's necessarily wonderful for the garden, except it does provide melting snow in the spring.

"There's nothing so bad, it isn't good for something," is what my mother used to say quite often. It applies to your garden as well! I try to keep it all as natural as possible. When I say I tend to be a "lazy gardener" that's what I mean! Let nature help in any way possible.

WATCHING THE BIRDS

Here I am at the window, counting chickadees and nuthatches again. It must be winter! I count birds for the "Cornell Project Feeder Watch" program. It increases my knowledge of the birds that visit our feeders. Since I started doing this, I know exactly how many of each species of bird come to my feeders through the winter. It's kind of fascinating to watch them. Counting them makes me so much more aware of whether I have a strange species, or if it's just my regular neighborhood flock.

It's a wonderful winter project for kids, as well as everyone else. Try it if you are interested, and perhaps join in the fun. There is a nominal fee that helps defray costs for the University, but it is SO worth it! You can find it on line by googling "Cornell Project Feeder Watch". Have fun!

SNOW IN THE FORECAST!

Well, it is finally arriving. I guess we cannot put it off any longer. Winter! At least the kids didn't have to ski around the neighborhood for their Halloween Trick or Treats! I guess that's a good thing! At any rate, welcome to the next season and "good night garden"! We all need time to recoup and regenerate, even the garden. In the tropics, this doesn't happen and I guess plants grow until they finally die of exhaustion. I know I would.

I have been enjoying the birds coming to the feeders. I have my feeders strung on a wire extended between the garage and the house. It's up high enough that the bears can't get to it. Today the birds seem extra ravenous. Maybe it's just the weather. I find that when the weather is supposed to be bad...they seem to know, and come to fill their tummies.

Bundle up and get a fire going in the fireplace. Got a good book to read? I do!

BULBS AND THEIR CARE

I just talked with our daughter, who had been out planting bulbs with her 5-year-old son. What fun! Can't you just imagine his joy in the spring when his bulbs come up and bloom? I can just picture him bringing in a bouquet for his Mom!

That brings up a good point about bulbs. This is the time when the bulbs in the ground are building up strength to last through the winter AND bulk up for spring bloom! If there is a bit of time you can give to your bulbs, now is it! Get out there and broadcast some slow acting fertilizer on the area where you have bulbs.

You'll be very happy you did come spring!

BIRD FEEDERS CAN SPREAD NOXIOUS WEEDS

Bird feeding is a popular fall and winter activity. We all love to watch the birds coming to our feeders. Feeding also helps birds survive the winter. However, we all know birds can be messy eaters. Much of the birdseed drops to the ground under the feeder. If the birds aren't dropping seeds, sometimes it's the squirrels invading the feeder. In either case, the seed that drops often germinates. While we'd like to think all the seed we buy for our birds is pure, research conducted at Oregon State University found the seed from 10 common brands of bird feed contained more than 50 noxious weed seeds as well. In the study, they found that 30 weed species, such as bindweed, velvetleaf, and ragweed, sprouted under bird feeders. These weeds can then spread to nearby fields and gardens.

You can't teach birds to be neater eaters, but there are ways to prevent these weeds from getting started. It is suggested using a tray under your feeder to keep the seeds off the ground and selecting bird food that won't sprout, such as sunflower hearts, peanut butter, raisins, mealworms, and plain suet cakes. Some seed manufacturers are now actually baking seeds before selling them to kill weed seeds. Look for baked wild bird seed at your garden center. Talk about "novel"!

RAIN, RAIN, DON'T GO AWAY!

Here it is November and it's pouring where we live. It's been pouring most of the night. DO NOT BEGRUDGE IT!

This is nature's way of taking care of trees and shrubs. Trees and shrubs need all the water they can store up before the frost gets so deep they get no more moisture. If they go into the winter "dry" it will be very stressful for them. That is why it's so important to water your shrubs and trees before winter really establishes itself.

In the spring the plants will have a HUGE job ahead of them. They will have lots of leaves and blossoms to generate. If they start thirsty and stressed, it only stands to reason that your show won't be as good. Then on top of that, if there's an onslaught of some kind of blight or insect infestation, just imagine how difficult that will be for them.

Stay ahead of this nasty curve and be sure your trees and shrubs always go into winter well hydrated! Mother Nature helps, but there's just so much nature can accomplish. Give a hand and water those trees and shrubs!

LOCAL FIRST

I went to a local Chamber of Commerce Breakfast meeting about "Local First".

Both local farmers and local restaurateurs had been invited. It was interesting to hear prospectives on both sides of this issue.

The goal is to hopefully have the restaurateurs buy their produce, dairy products and meat from local farmers. This benefits the farmers with a market; it benefits the restaurants with fresh, locally grown food; it enables the restaurants to feel good about what they are feeding their customers while supporting the local farmers who will also choose to eat at these restaurants.

Part of the issue is that buying from big producers is inexpensive, while local farmers tend to charge more. The quality is far superior at the local farms, but the prices need to be reasonable. If the higher costs are passed on to the consumers, they will find another place to eat. Restaurateurs can absorb some of the cost, but it needs to be reasonable.

So, the object is to help both farmers and restaurateurs come to an agreement that is beneficial for both parties.

It was one of our better meetings as far as the transfer of ideas and concerns between parties.

CAN I STILL PLANT SPRING BULBS?

Sure, you can still plant bulbs! As long as the ground is not frozen, it will work.

I'm seeing a lot of sales advertizing bulbs. Take advantage of those sales. You'll be planting the bulbs pretty much below the frost level. They will work on building roots and a larger bulb all winter and reward you in the spring.

Go ahead and splurge! Get some wonderful bulbs. You'll be glad you did come spring.

GARDENING CHORES FOR NOVEMBER

- Now's the time to plant **paperweight narcissus, hyacinths and amaryllis (indoors)** for beautiful color and aroma on New Year's Day!

- If you've had enough freezing days to render the ground hard, begin to mulch **roses** and other shrubs, etc.

- **Fertilize the area where you have your bulbs.** It will sink into the soil gradually and be taken up by the bulbs.

- Put **wire guards, or wrap specially designed** to prevent mouse damage, around the bases of tree trunks .

- Wrap plants in **burlap** for winter protection. **Do NOT use plastic!** They can't breathe any better inside plastic than you can.

- **Yank out the annuals**-or cut them back at ground level, leaving the roots to decompose.

- If you haven't **fertilized** your lawn or garden yet, now's the time!

- Use **anti-desiccant** to prevent loss of water during the long winter, if you haven't already.

- It's a good idea to be sure your **power equipment** works properly. Now is a good time to take them to the shop for repairs and upkeep.

- **Add leaves**, and the last bits of cut grass, to the compost

- **Turn the compost** one last time

- **Cover that compost** heap or bin with plastic to keep the nutrients from being leached out from winter rain and snow. (If you will be adding wood ashes to the compost during the winter, forgo the cover!)

- **Water your trees and shrubs** right up until the ground freezes.

- Check those trees and shrubs for **diseased foliage** and remove it. Remember **anything diseased should go into the garbage, NOT the compost**.

- If you have any **left over bulbs**, for goodness sake **PLANT THEM NOW**!!! (Assuming you live where the ground is still soft enough to plant!)

- Are you going to have a **live Christmas tree**? Dig the hole now, then cover the hole (and the dirt you removed) so you can easily plant it after the holidays.

- **Start feeding the birds**, if you haven't already.

THE DECEMBER GARDEN

BIG SNOW STORM COMING

I'm ready! Are you?

The big question is, are our gardens are ready? As the saying goes "ready or not, here it comes".

What goes on under all that snow and frost? Are all the little critters hunkering down for a long winters nap? Nope, they're planning how to get food to sustain them through the winter. They are eyeing your shrubs and tender, little trees. The bark is SOOOO inviting. Yum! If you haven't put some protection around the lower trunks, they will burrow right up to that yummy green bark and proceed to happily chew away!

Hopefully, you thought about that back in the fall. It's important. You can lose a lot of good trees, vines, and shrubs that way.

REMOVAL OF SNOW ON BROADLEAF EVERGREENS

Have you gotten a nice heavy coating of snow yet?

When you are out shoveling, or sweeping, blowing, or whatever you do with new snow, remember to give your broadleaf evergreen shrubs a bit of attention. That snow looks very pretty, but it is very hard on the shrubs. If it's a light dusting, there's no problem, but when we get a heavy snow cover that piles up on those leaves it's a disaster waiting to happen. You'll notice that the branches are weighed down, drooping almost to the ground. Imagine if that were your arms having to hold onto all that heavy stuff!

When you see branches heavy-laden with snow, poke the handle end of a broom, or shovel into the bush pushing the branches gently to dislodge the snow, so it spills to the ground. The branches will pop up gratefully! If you don't do this, the next thing that happens is a thaw (usually); the snow begins to melt; then evening comes and the temperature drops causing that wet snow to freeze. The problem is exacerbated. Now it's heavier, impossible to remove and branches begin to break at the slightest disturbance!

Once ice has formed, I would suggest that you forgo this process because when you push on the branches they will more than likely break. Leave them alone and hope for the best!

Remember, in nature, bushes and trees don't have someone doing this for them. It's a kind of natural pruning technique...but not one that is particularly neat, or good for the plant! Broken branches, besides looking bad, are magnets for disease and insect "invasion".

Go through this process with all your broad-leaved evergreens, or at least those with which you are concerned. Sometimes, I realize they are too big, or not easily accessed. Use your judgment.

As far as the garden is concerned, the snow provides a good, stabilizing cover for everything. It acts as mulch, protecting the ground from the fluctuating temperatures. That's a good thing. The bad thing about this much snow is that it can, as mentioned, become a very heavy burden for trees and shrubs. The branches are often pushed to their breaking point and hence we see a lot of broken branches in the spring. We can help with this. It's a good thing for us to get out into the fresh air anyway, so let's be productive when we can.

As you can see, we should not ignore the garden entirely during winter. It will still benefit from our stewardship!

YOUR NEW AMARYLLIS BULB!

It's that time of year again. People give, get or just buy an amaryllis bulb for themselves. The pictures are beautiful. The ones you see at friend's houses always look absolutely breathtaking! So, why not give it a try? Here are some hints to help you get started.

First of all, think of the amaryllis bulb like an onion. You wouldn't buy a soft onion. Don't buy a soft amaryllis either! It should be firm and just LOOK good! Also, the larger it is, the more spectacular the bloom.

Lot's of bulbs that you plant in the garden need to be chilled before you plant them in the garden. Remember, an amaryllis is not a hardy bulb. It normally grows in a warmer climate, so chilling it is not at all helpful. In fact, it could be harmful. Try not to get it any colder than about 50 degrees.

The bulb should be well watered when you start it. After that's done you won't need to be quite so attentive with water. It shouldn't dry out, but remember that sitting in water will cause it to rot.

The bulb will generate some roots, so the pot

should be larger than the bulb. Also, once the bulb begins to grow, it will become tall and heavy. This means that you need to offset that weight. I'd use a clay pot and perhaps one that's not tall, but rather low and broad. This would also indicate that a very light potting medium might not be the best. Use a heavier soil.

You shouldn't have to fertilize the bulb. If you recall from your daffodils, tulips and other garden bulbs, they get their nutrients from their leaves as they die down. This tells you that the bulb has already taken what it needs from its leaves after the last flowering.

After it's potted, you can put it right into a sunny window. Unlike paper-whites, it doesn't need a period of darkness to spur it onward. Don't forget that a plant will lean toward the light. If this begins to happen, rotate the pot daily.

After you've attended to all of this, it should take about 6-10 weeks for you to see a bud, followed by a beautiful show!

GARDENING CHORES FOR DECEMBER

- If you haven't yet, and still can, dig a hole in which you can place your live **holiday tree** after Christmas. Store the soil you dig out in the garage, or other non-frozen place so you can just dump it into the hole after the tree is planted!

- Have you made **"tee-pee's" to cover your smaller shrubs**, protecting them from **snow loads**? Be sure they are out in the garden, doing their job! You can also wrap the plants, or shrubs in burlap.

- Plant your **pre-cooled bulbs** in pots for some wonderful indoor color. Put them first in a cool and dark spot to begin growing roots, and water them, so they don't dry out.

- Remove decorative foil from **gift plants**. Set the plants into waterproof containers, after placing a layer of gravel in the bottom (of the outside container) so the plant doesn't sit in water. Indoor plants are harmed more by too MUCH water, rather than too little!

- **Poinsettias** should be in moist, NOT wet soil.

- Fertilize **houseplants**.

- If you haven't done it yet, put **stakes** around your gardens bordering driveways and roads where plowed snow might harm them. The stakes will guide the plow elsewhere!

- Save **hardwood ashes** to amend the soil in the spring. **If your compost pile is not covered**, the ashes can go right in there.

- Think about purchasing gardening tools, equipment, and books as **Christmas gifts**.

- Go to a **gardening seminar**.

- **Take a gardening break!**

A VERY BASIC VOCABULARY LIST FOR A BEGINNING GARDENER

This is the most basic vocabulary you'll ever need. If you want something that isn't listed here, you can always refer to a standard dictionary or gardening book.

- **aeration**-supplying the soil with air in one way or another.
- **alpine**- a plant native to alpine regions
- **amendments**-something that is added to soil in order to improve its texture or fertility
- **annual**- a plant that completes it's life cycle in one growing season
- **biennials**- continuing or lasting for two years; or growing leaves and roots during the first year, then fruiting and dying during the second year
- **bract**-usually a small, leaf-like structure found below a flower. They are often confused with the petals of a flower. For instance, the large red, or white "leaves" on a poinsettia are "bracts", not flowers.
- **brambles**- usually prickly shrubs including raspberries and blackberries
- **bulb**- a rounded underground storage organ present in some plants
- **compost**- a mixture that consists largely of decayed organic matter. It is used for fertilizing and conditioning soil
- **corm**- A short thick solid food-storing underground stem, sometimes bearing papery scale leaves, as in gladiolus
- **cultivate**- To loosen or dig soil around growing plants

- **Deadheading**-removing old flowers during the growing season to encourage the development of new flowers and to prevent seed formation. Deadheading also improves the appearance of the garden. On the down side, removing seed heads may also mean depriving seed-eating birds of a favorite food—and depriving the gardener of the company of the birds.
- **division**- A type of propagation characteristic of plants that spread by means of newly formed parts such as bulbs, suckers, or rhizomes.
- **dormant oil spray**-is oil suspended in an emulsion. It is used mostly in orchards to control sucking insects.
- **evergreen**- having foliage that remains green and functional through the winter. The plant does NOT die back.
- **fertilizer**- a substance (either organic or chemical) used to make soil more fertile
- **forcing**- bringing plants to maturity out of it's normal season, as in forcing lilies for Easter
- **frost**- temperature that causes freezing, and hence the death of tender plants.
- **fungus**- plants that lack chlorophyll and include molds, rusts, mildews, mushrooms, and yeast
- **genus**-a class of things that have common characteristics
- **germination**-begins when the seedlings first appear at the surface of the soil, or when the first tiny roots appear.
- **graft**-a shoot or twig inserted into a slit on the trunk or stem of a living plant, from which it receives sap, and continues to grow i n it's new location.

- **granite dust**- granite stone meal which is a natural source of potash. It is cheaper than chemical potash fertilizers, and leaves no harmful chemicals.
- **green manure**-a cover crop which provides a vegetative cover protecting topsoil from wind and water erosion. It is then usually tilled into the soil providing additional fertility.
- **ground covers**-low-growing, spreading plants that help to crowd weeds out of the garden.
- **guano**-the droppings of birds and bat colonies. It is very fertile.
- **hardiness**-refers to climatic conditions of the particular area where a plant is to placed. Most gardening catalogues and gardening books have "hardiness maps" to help you in the purchase of proper plants for your zone.
- **heavy soil**-contains a lot of silt and clay, generally holding too much water and having poor drainage.
- **heeling-in**-the practice of covering plant roots temporarily with soil before actually planting them.
- **humus**-fully broken down compost.
- **hydroponics**-the art of growing vegetables in water.
- **insecticide**-a substance that is toxic to insects
- **irrigation**-keeping moisture in contact with plant roots
- **layering**- a method of propagation where an attached stem of a living shrub is put into the ground and allowed to root. Usually the stem is held in contact with the soil by a stone or other means of restraint.
- **legume**-a plant that has "pods", like a pea or bean. They have the ability to fix nitrogen from the air into the soil. They are good for soil building, and

as use for foraging.
- **lime**-is used as an alkalizer to raise the pH of the soil.
- **loam**-this is a mixture of soil that contains clay, silt, and sand, as well as organic matter.
- **manure**-barnyard "excreta"! Be careful to compost this before applying to your garden. It can be quite "hot" and can burn your plants. When it is applied, dig it into the soil to avoid having it wash off the surface.
- **manure tea**-make just like regular tea, except use manure instead of tea leaves! Add water, allow it to steep, and use it to water your plants. You can use compost as well, creating "compost tea".
- **Milky Spore disease**-a bacterial disease, which is used to control Japanese (and other) beetles.
- **mulch**-a material you put on top of the soil around your plants to hold in moisture. It could be compost, plastic, or shredded rubber
- **nematode**-a very tiny worm found in soil everywhere. They can be harmful to the root systems of plants, although there are also good nematodes.
- **nitrogen**-element necessary for plant growth, which shows above the ground (think "grass")
- **node**- where a bud originates on a stem.
- **organic matter**-derived from living matter like leaves, plants, and even animal remains. Anything that has been alive is considered to be organic matter in the garden.
- **ornamental plant**-grown for it's looks, rather than consumption
- **pathogen**-micro-organism that can cause disease
- **peat**-boggy, acid ground, consisting of partly decomposed vegetable matter. It is often used as a

soil amendment.
- **perennial**-any plant that lives longer than two years. It generally refers to herbaceous plants, rather than trees and shrubs.
- **pesticide**-any chemical substance used to kill animal and insect pests.
- **pH**-a measure of acidity and alkalinity that is a number on a scale where 7 represents neutrality. Lower numbers indicate increasing acidity and higher numbers increasing alkalinity
- **phosphorus**-a major element in plant nutrition. It supplies food to roots, fruit as well as helping with disease resistance
- **pinching**- to prune the tip of a plant or shoot, usually to induce branching
- **pollinator**- an insect that pollinates flowers
- **potash**-another important plant nutrient, also called potassium oxide. It helps the plant resist disease, while helping to protect them during drought and cold.
- **potassium**-also called potash
- **propagation**-reproduction of plant
- **pruning**-to cut off or cut back parts of a bush or tree to create a more pleasing shape, or to remove dead or diseased branches on a shrub or tree. It is also done to limit growth, allowing sun to penetrate to the interior of the plant. It can be helpful to keep a plant's overall growth in check, while keeping it attractive in appearance. There are other reasons as well, but these will do for now. This is a topic to fill a book!
- **pruning saw**- A saw with a relatively long and narrow cutting blade that can get into tight places

- **Rain Garden**-essentially a backyard "wetland" having a shallow basin depth, gentle side slopes, soil that allows infiltration, and vegetation that traps sediment and sediment-polluting runoff.
- **rhizomes**- a somewhat long usually horizontal subterranean plant stem that is often thickened by deposits of reserve food material. It produces shoots above and roots below, and is distinguished from a true root in that it has buds and nodes, as in an iris.
- **rock garden**- a garden planned around natural rock formations or rocks artificially arranged to simulate natural (often mountainous) conditions
- **rotation**- Rotation is a gardening practice where different vegetable plants are placed in a different section of the garden each year.
- **seedling**-a very young plant that sprouts from a seed.
- **separating**-a version of propagation when plants are divided
- **shrub**- a low usually several-stemmed woody plant
- **side dress**-to place plant nutrients (usually fertilizer) near, or above, the roots of a growing plant.
- **Soft wood cuttings**-cutting the very newest, tender branches of a tree or shrub, and plunging them into a planting medium, and encouraging them to sprout roots. This is a form of propagation.
- **soil**-the top layer of the earth's surface in which the roots of plants develop. It provides the plants with the necessary nutrients, water and gases. There are many more things in soil, but this is enough for now.
- **succulents**- Having thick, fleshy, water-storing leaves or stems

- **sucker**- a shoot from the roots or lower part of the stem of a plant
- **tender**- sensitive to frost or severe cold. The opposite of hardy
- **transplant**- to lift and reset (a plant) in another place
- **variegated**- leaves having streaks, marks, or patches of a different color or colors
- **viability**-the point at which a plant can thrive on it's own.
- **water garden**- Any ornamental tub, pool, or other natural or artificial water container planted with aquatic plants.
- **water shoots or sprouts**-fast growing, upright and straight succulent stems that do NOT bear fruit and are generally a negative factor in any shrub or tree. They should be pruned out.
- **weed**-any plant growing where it's NOT wanted
- **Xeriscape**-a landscaping method that utilizes water-conserving methods. This can be used in ANY horticultural zone.
- **zone**- The contiguous United States and southern Canada are divided into 10 zones based on a 10 F (5.6 C) difference in average annual minimum temperature.

Average Annual Extreme Minimum Temperature 1976-2005

Temp (F)	Zone	Temp (C)
-60 to -50	1	-51.1 to -45.6
-50 to -40	2	-45.6 to -40
-40 to -30	3	-40 to -34.4
-30 to -20	4	-34.4 to -28.9
-20 to -10	5	-28.9 to -23.3
-10 to 0	6	-23.3 to -17.8
0 to 10	7	-17.8 to -12.2
10 to 20	8	-12.2 to -6.7
20 to 30	9	-6.7 to -1.1
30 to 40	10	-1.1 to 4.4
40 to 50	11	4.4 to 10
50 to 60	12	10 to 15.6
60 to 70	13	15.6 to 21.1

ABOUT THE AUTHOR

Annemarie Godston is the author of a number of gardening blogs. She was certified as a Master Gardener in Connecticut and New Hampshire.

In New Hampshire she served on the Grafton County University of New Hampshire Extension Board for three years, before moving to Seattle, WA.

While in New Hampshire, she also taught gardening classes for the Dartmouth College ILEAD (Institute of Lifelong Education At Dartmouth) Program.

Made in the USA
Charleston, SC
23 March 2015